Beginner Math Workbook For Preschool

(Pre-K Edition)

Speedy Publishing LLC
40 E. Main St. #1156
Newark, DE 19711
www.speedypublishing.com

Practice Tracing Numbers

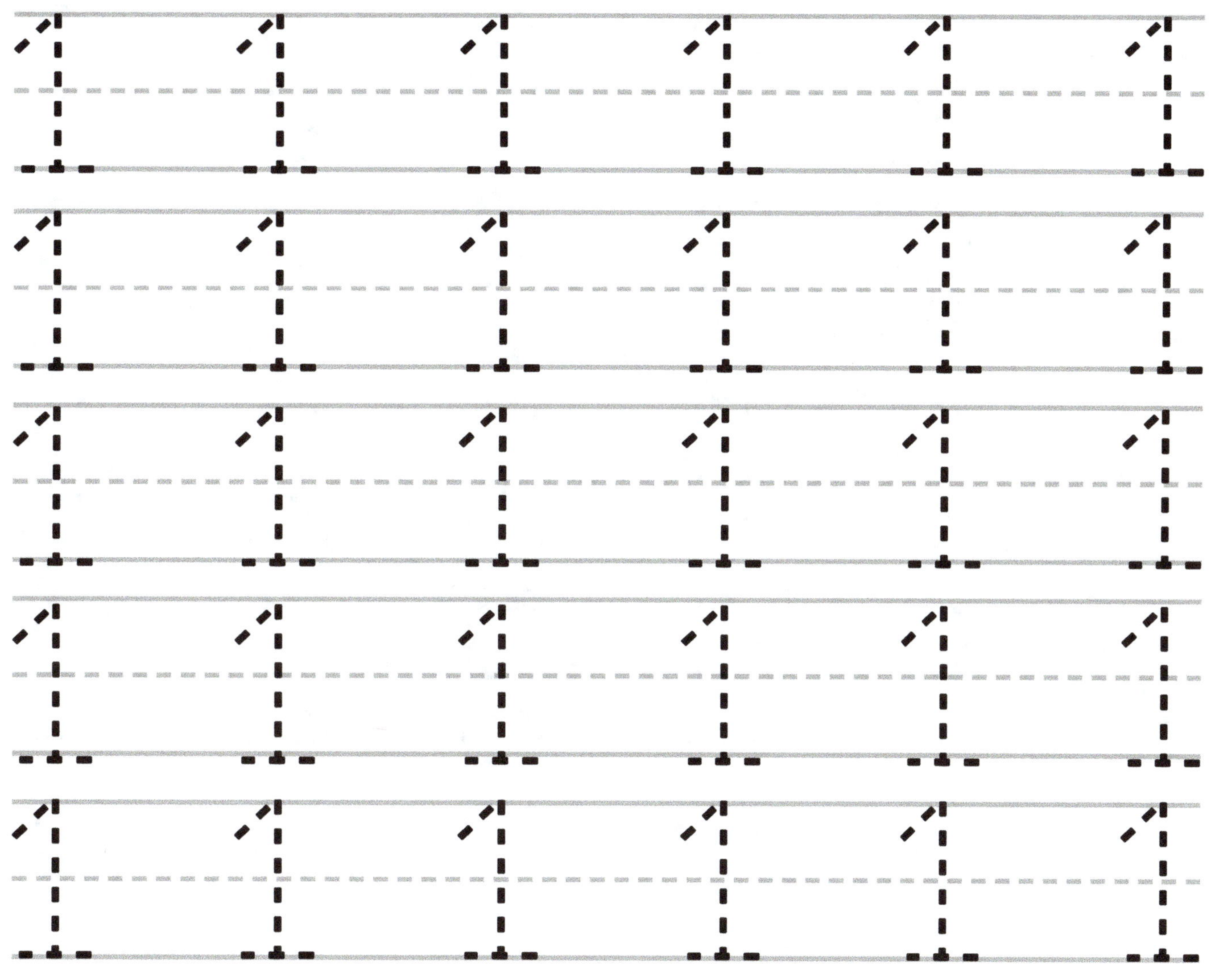

Practice Tracing Numbers

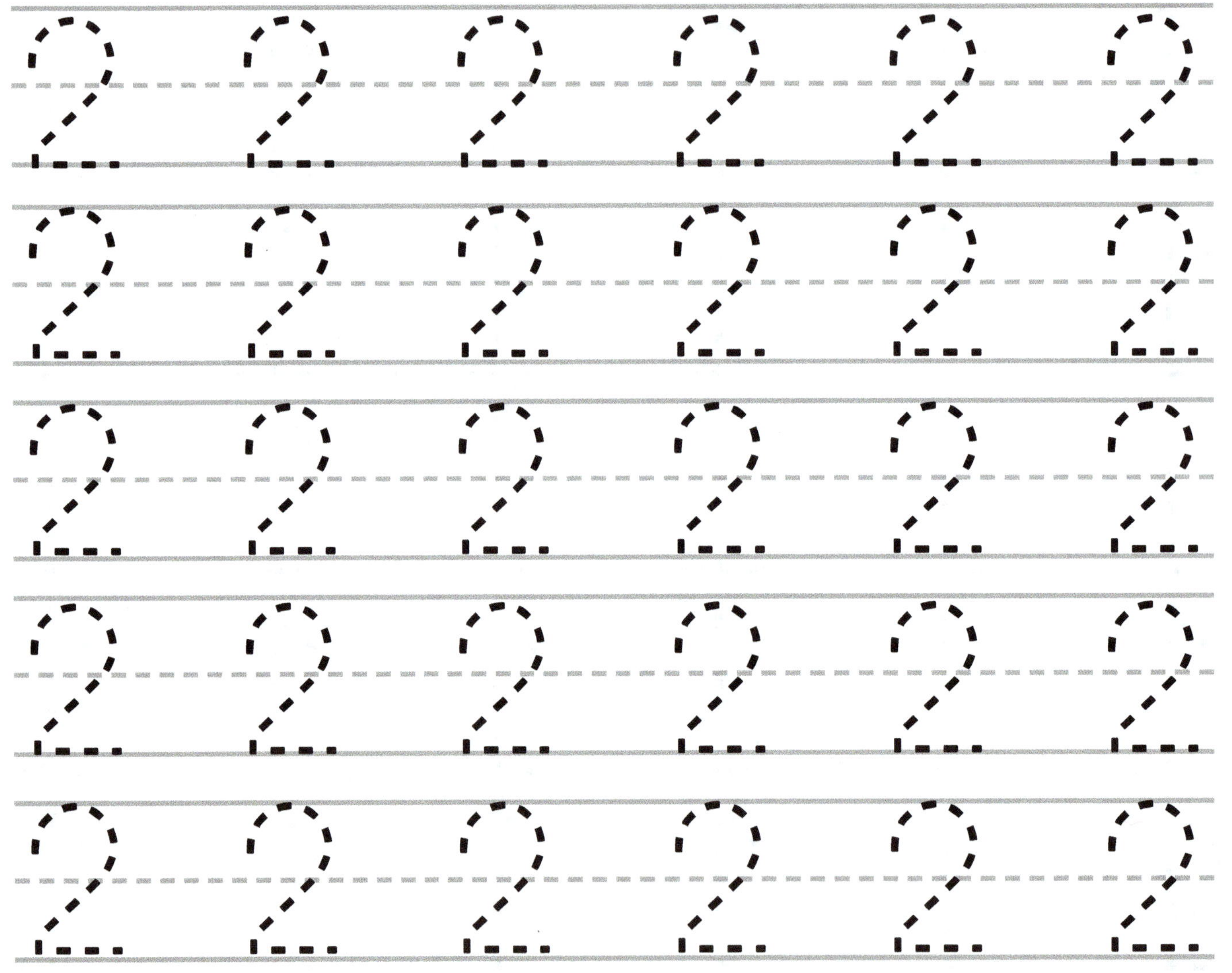

Practice Tracing Numbers

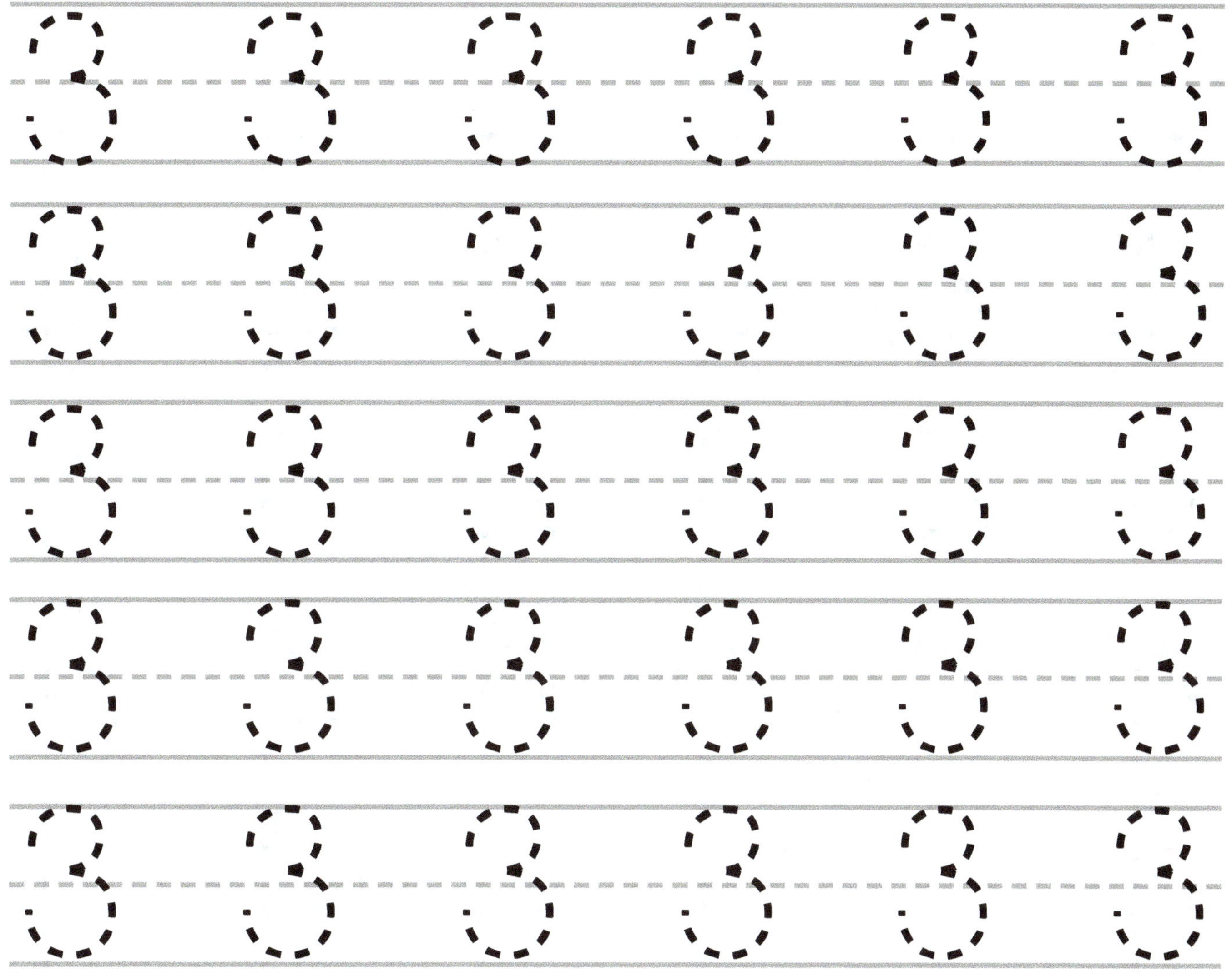

Practice Tracing Numbers

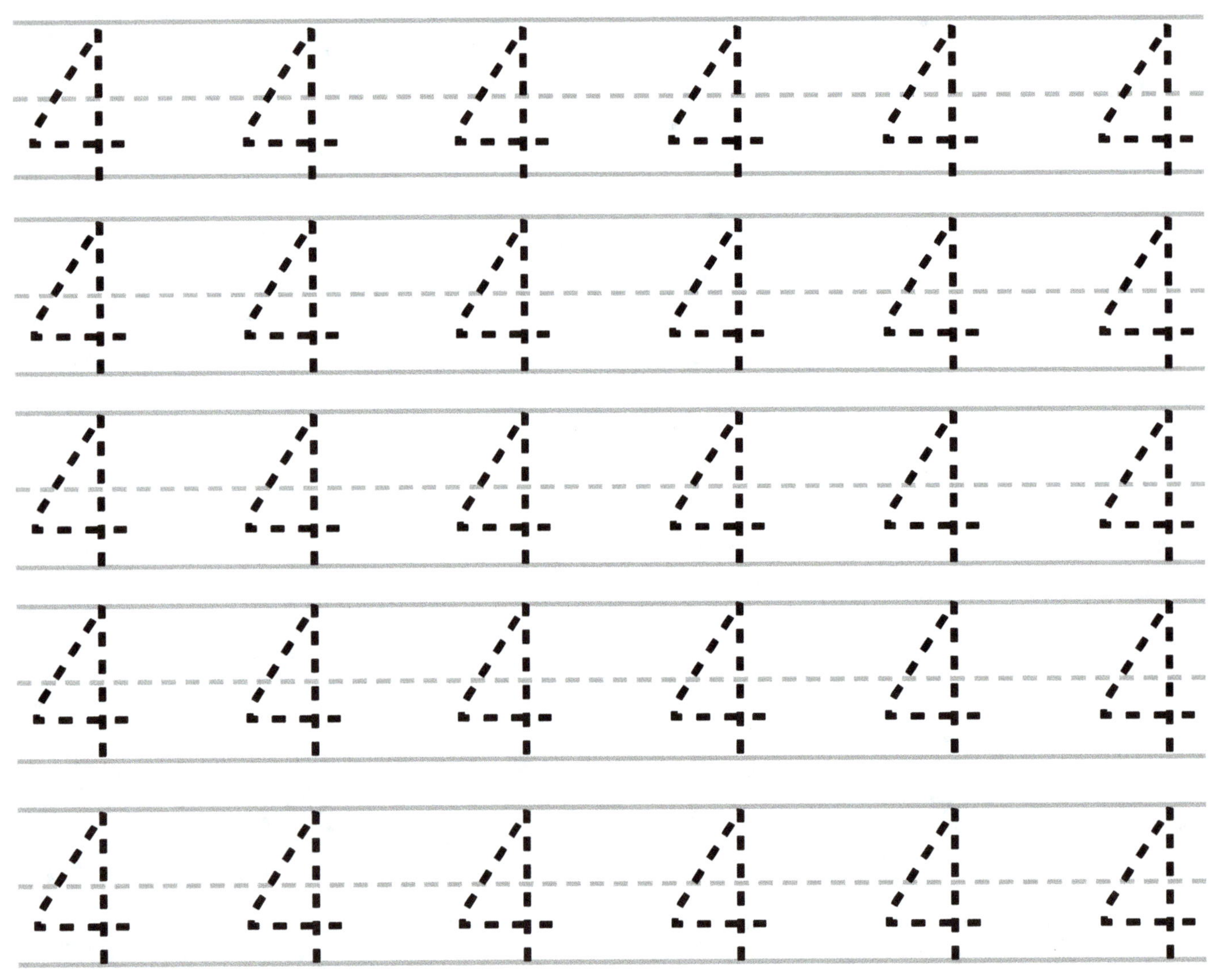

Practice Tracing Numbers

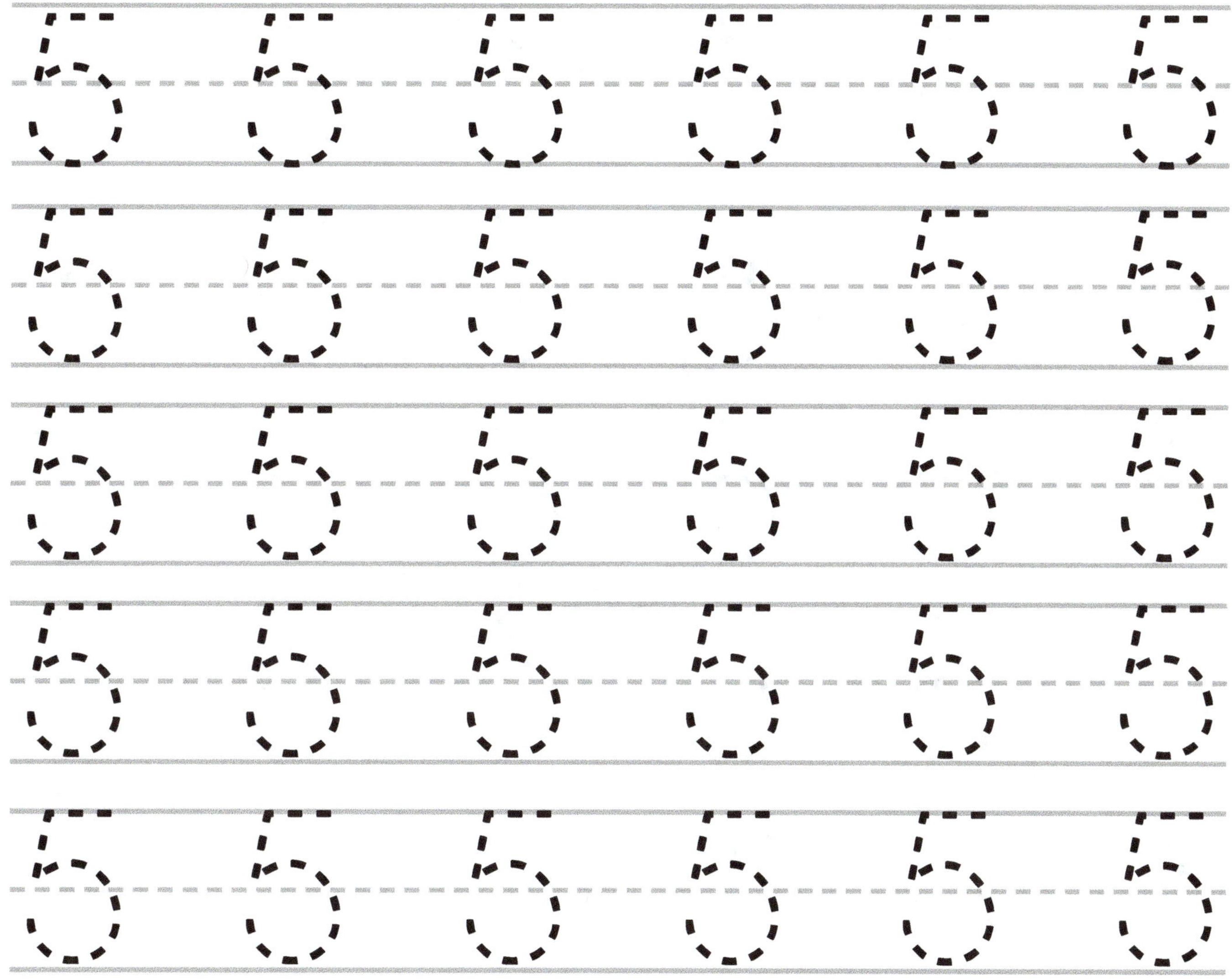

Practice Tracing Numbers

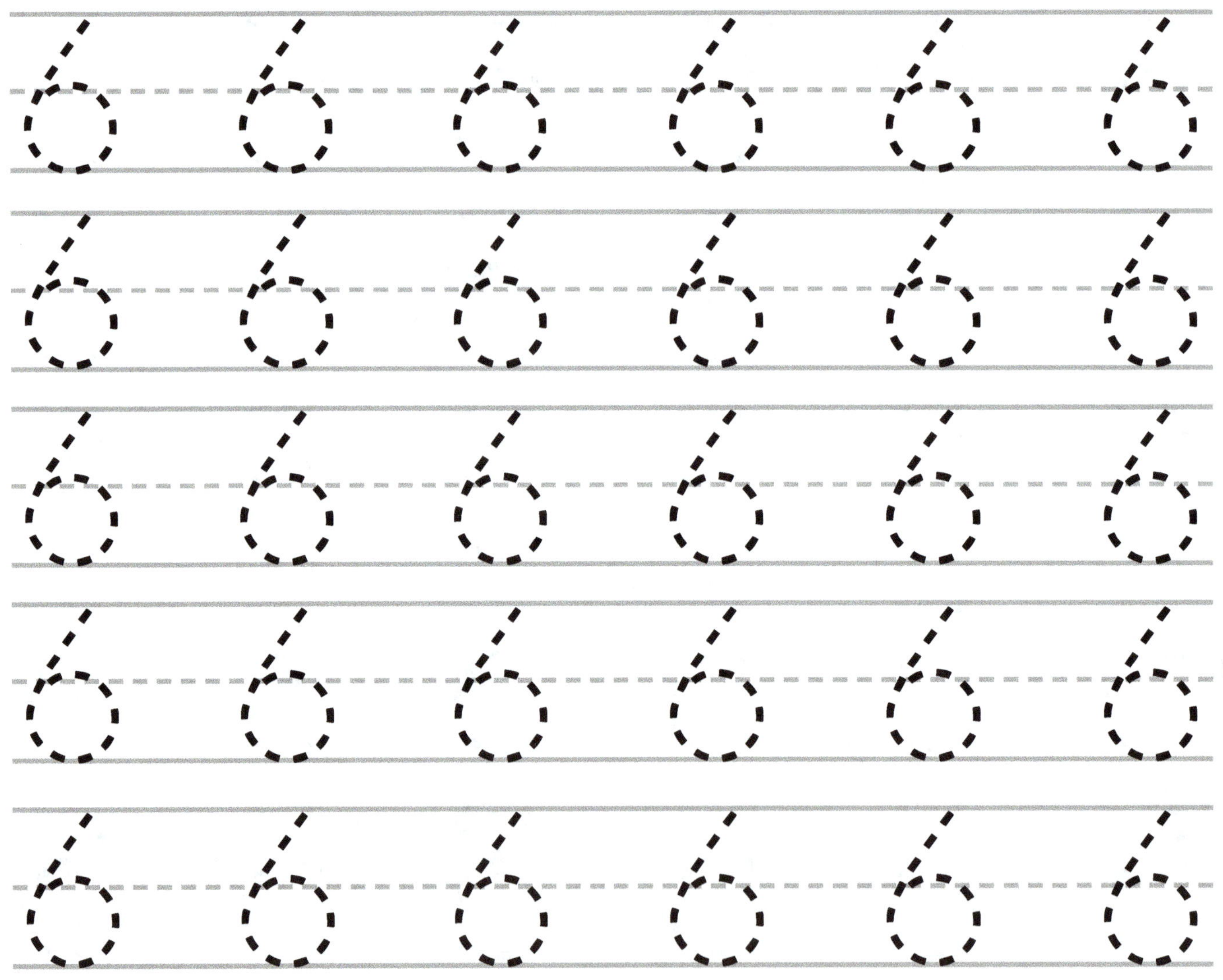

Practice Tracing Numbers

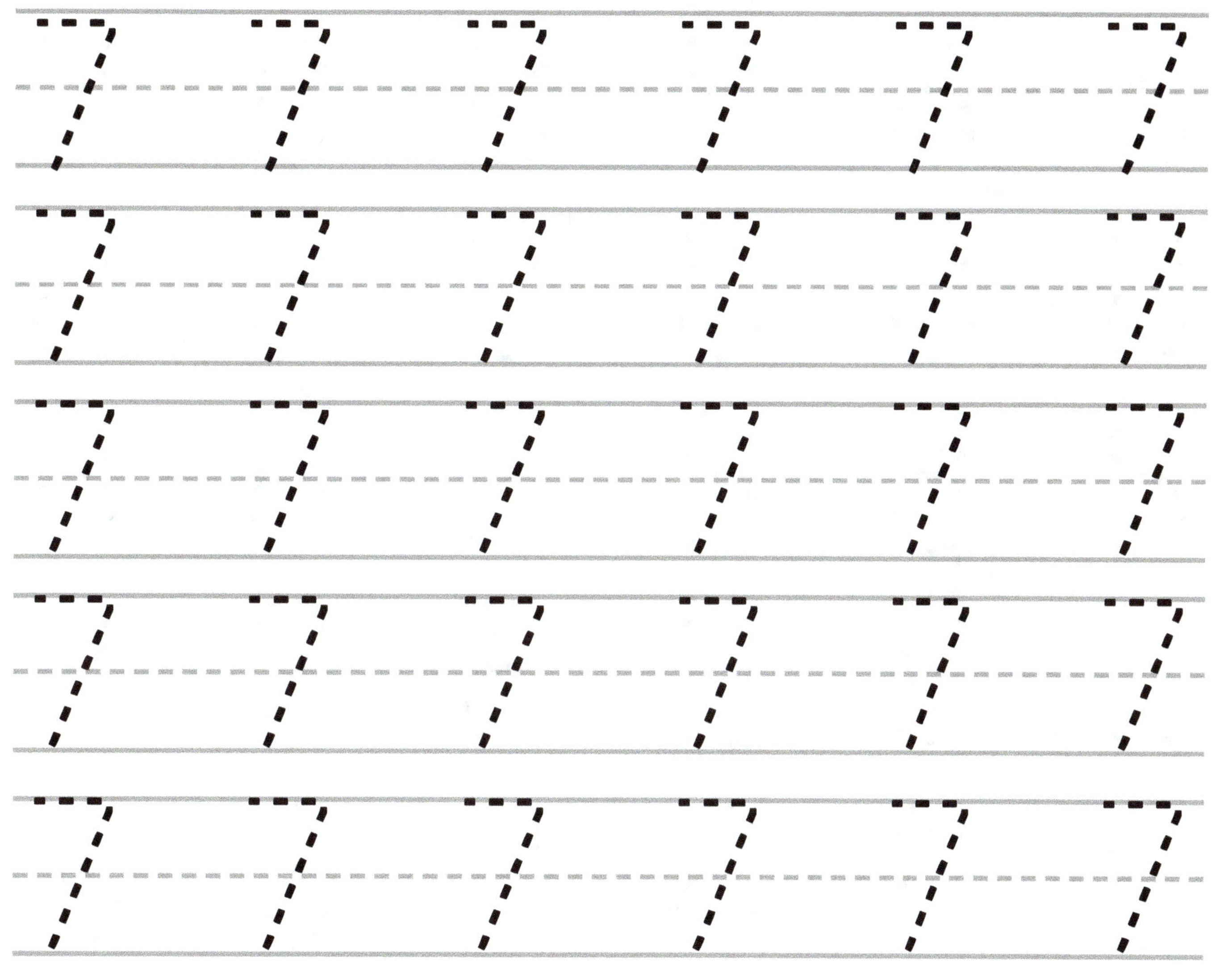

Practice Tracing Numbers

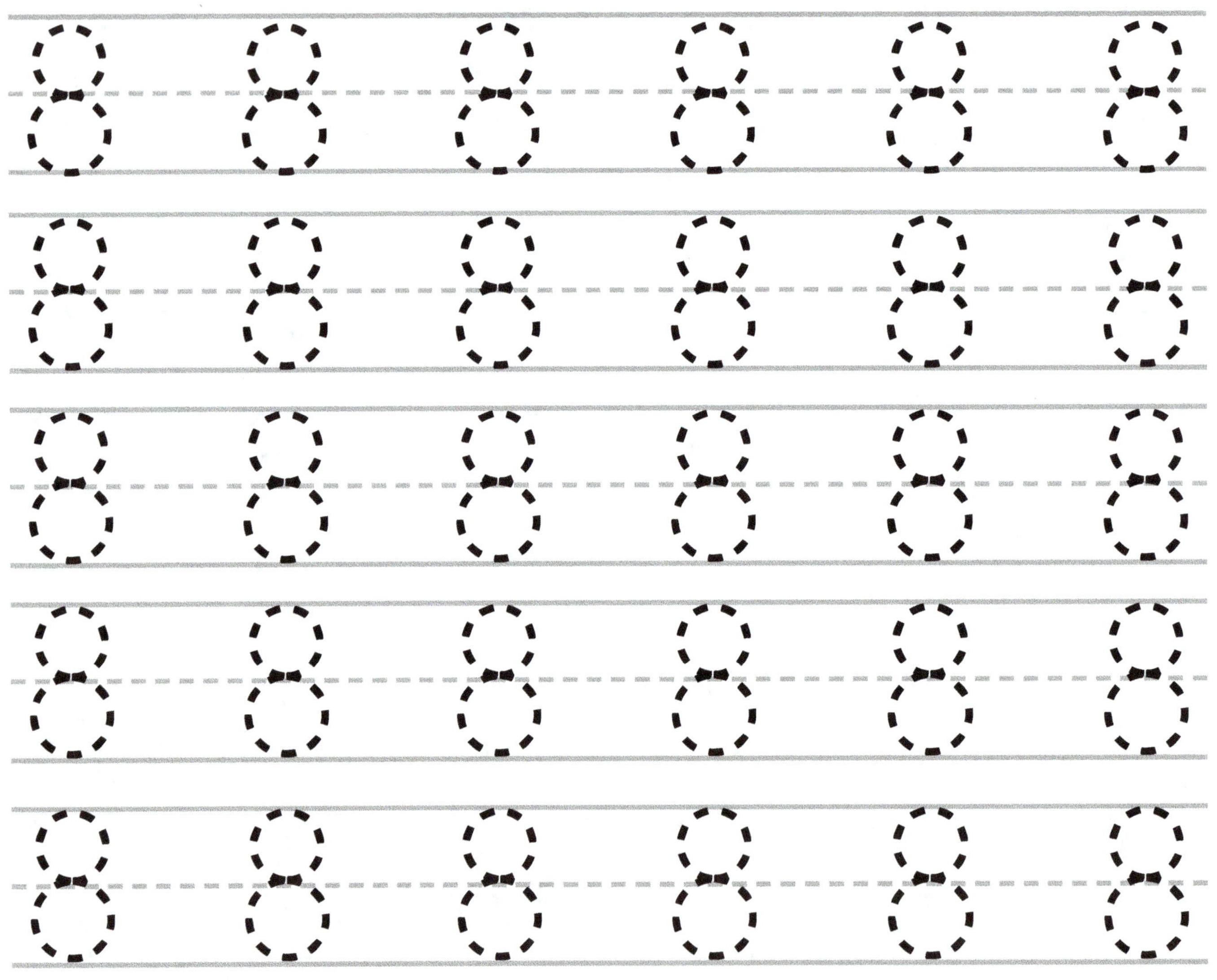

Practice Tracing Numbers

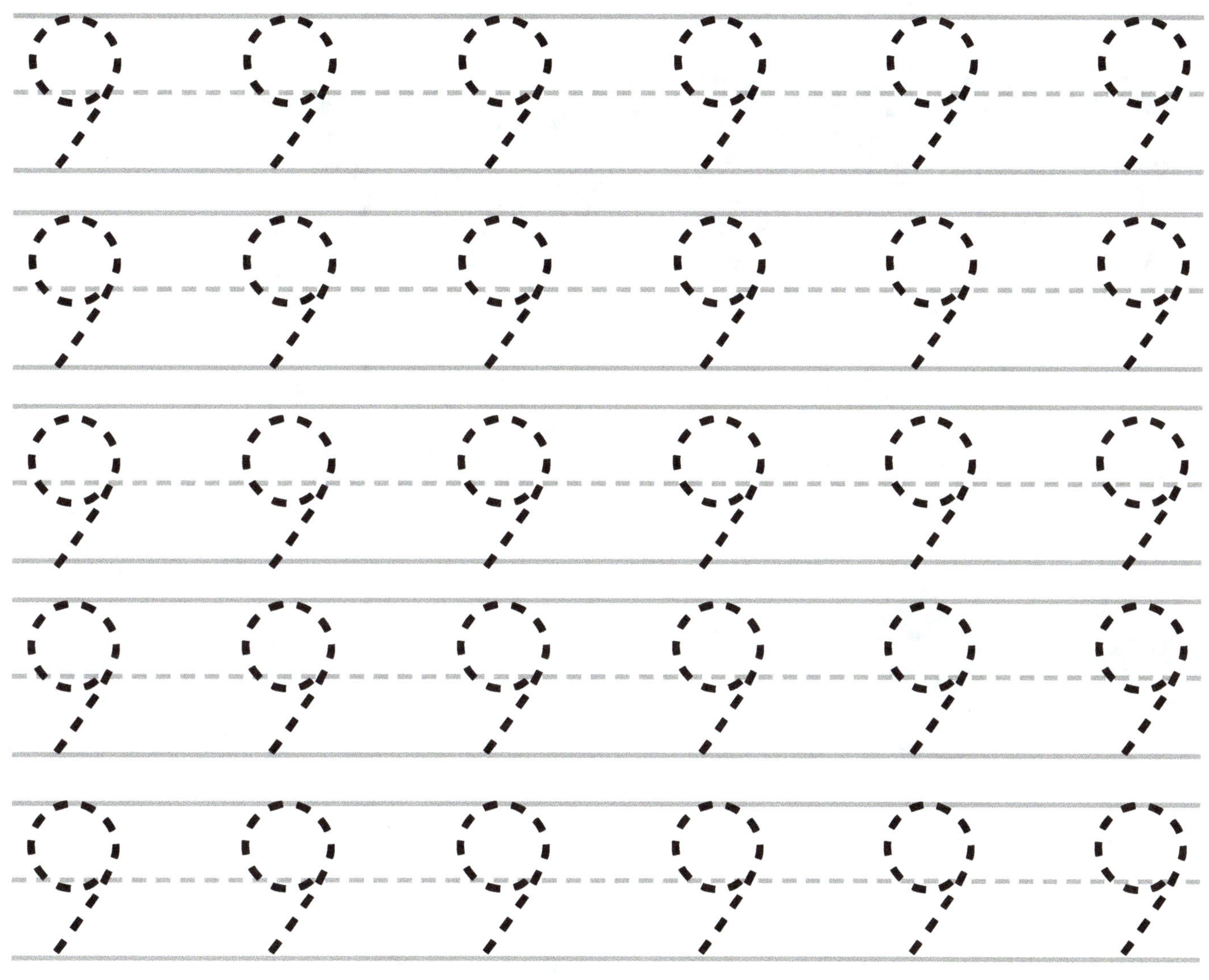

Counting objects

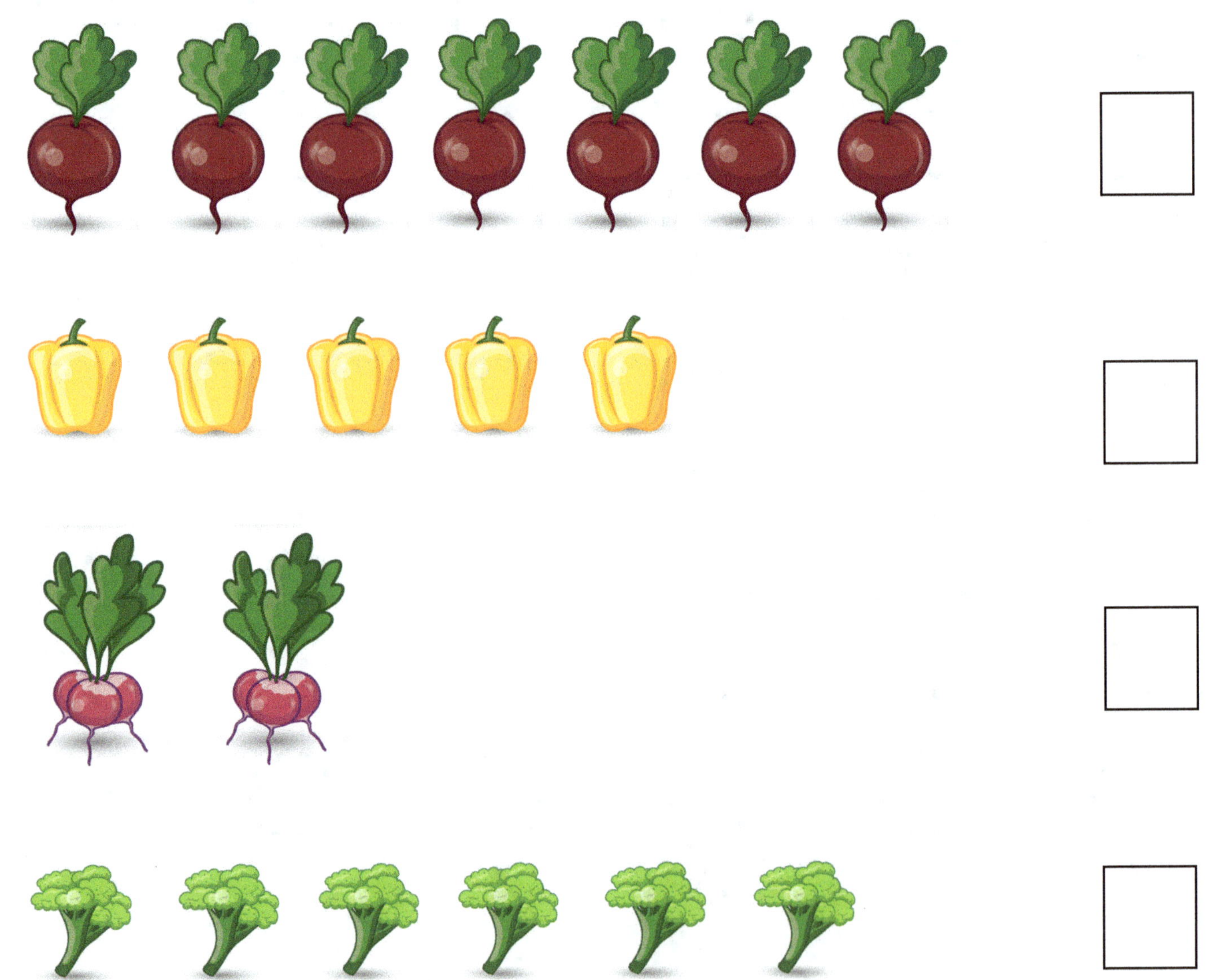

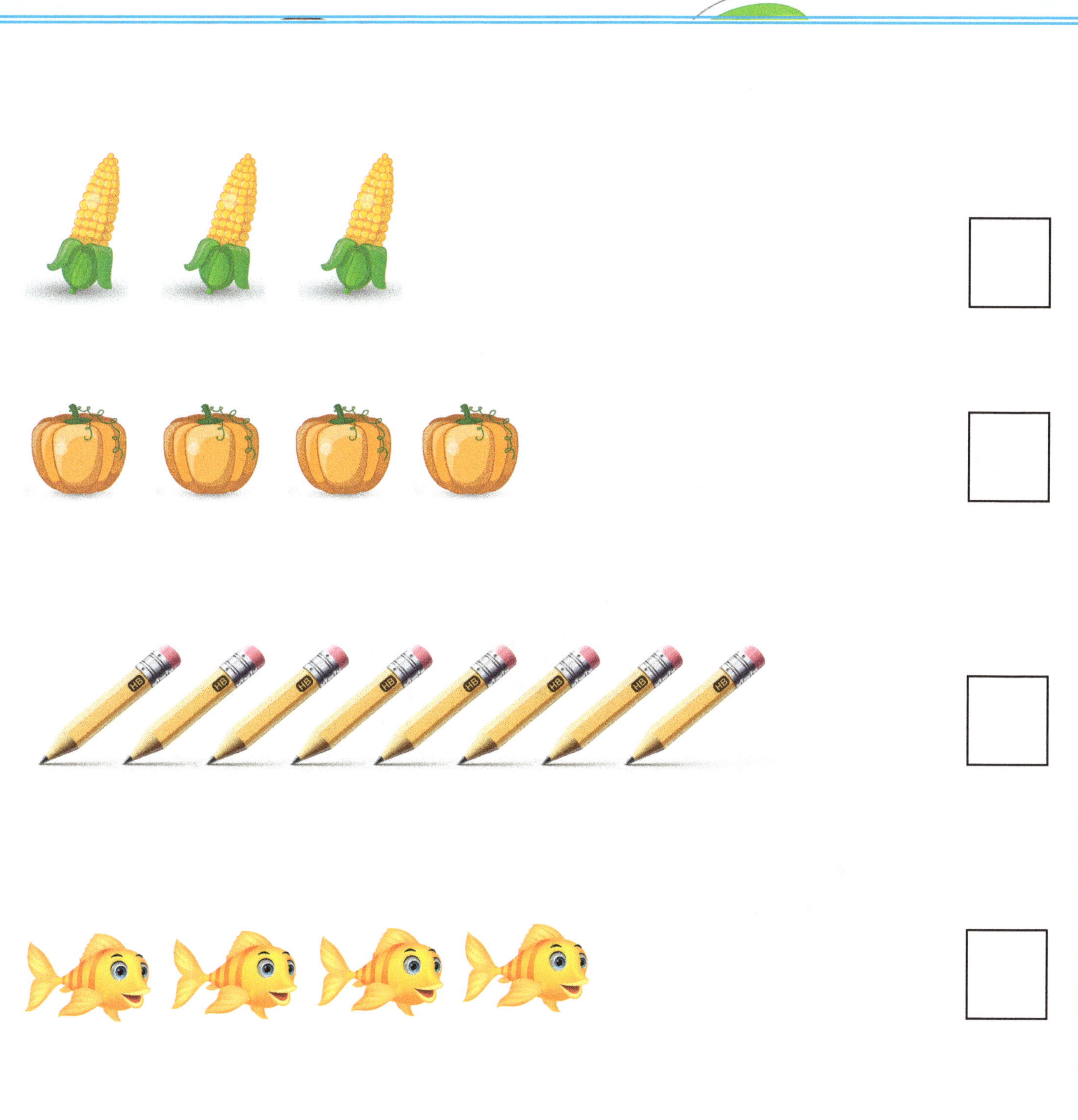

How many tomatoes are there?

How many apples are there?

How many bell peppers are there?

How many ducks are there?

How many rabbits are there?

Count the dots and add them.

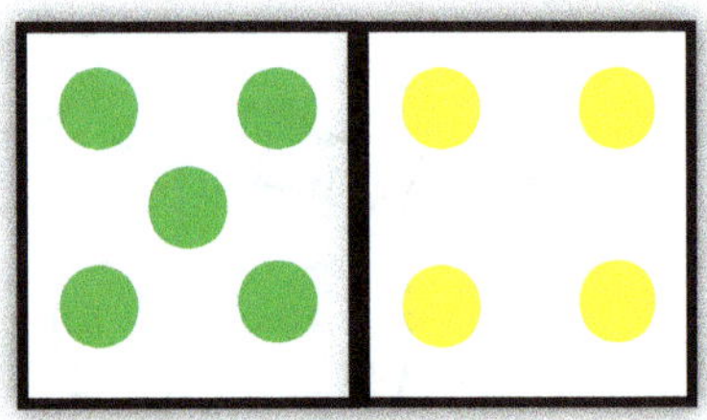

$\underline{5} + \underline{4} = 9$

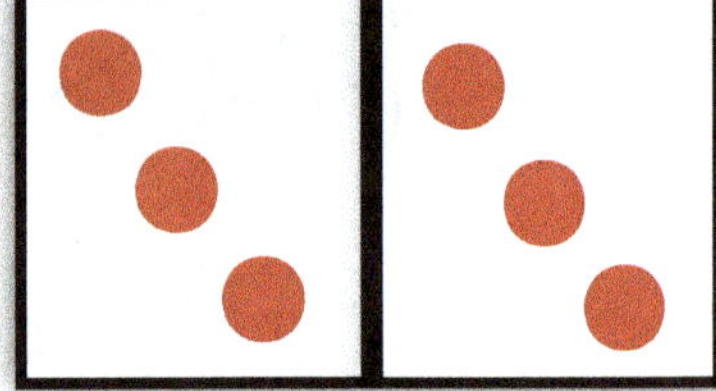

$\_\_\_ + \_\_\_ =$

$\_\_\_ + \_\_\_ =$

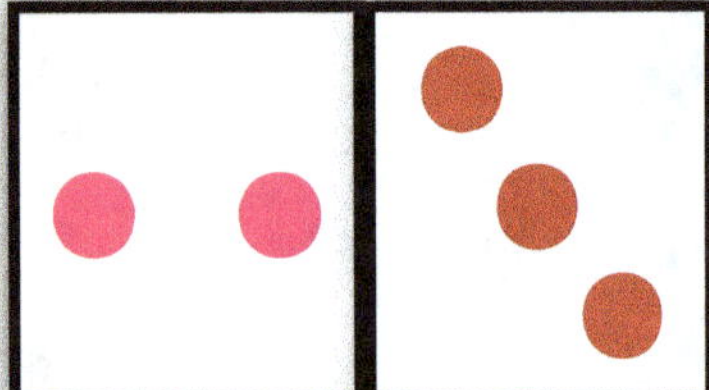

$\_\_\_ + \_\_\_ =$

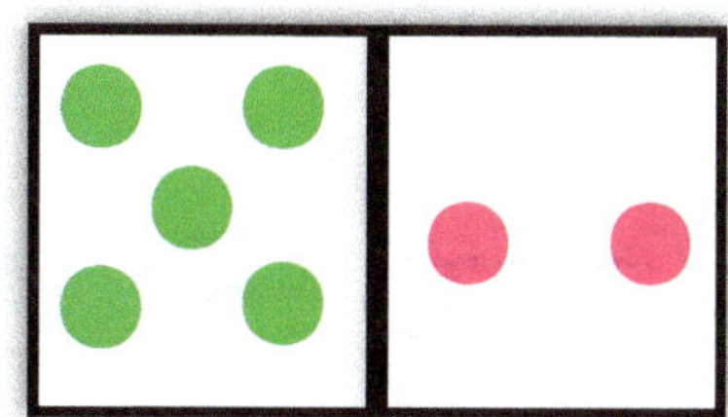

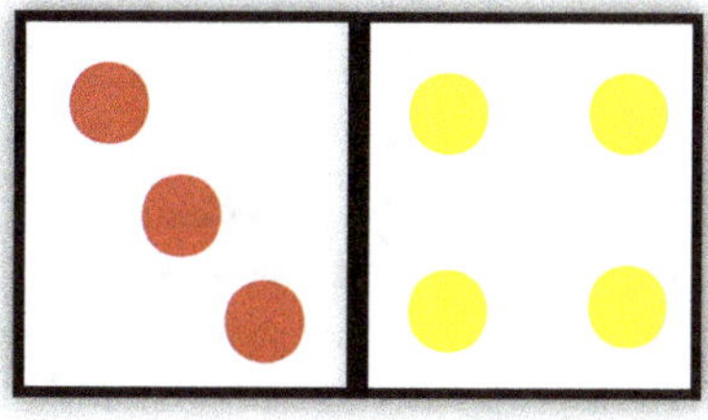

___ + ___ =

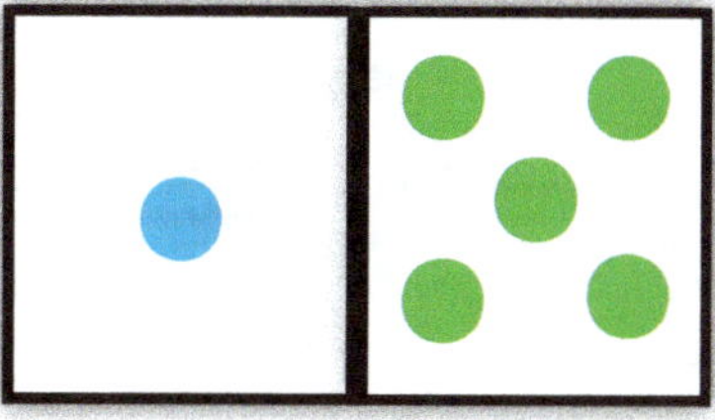

___ + ___ =

___ + ___ =

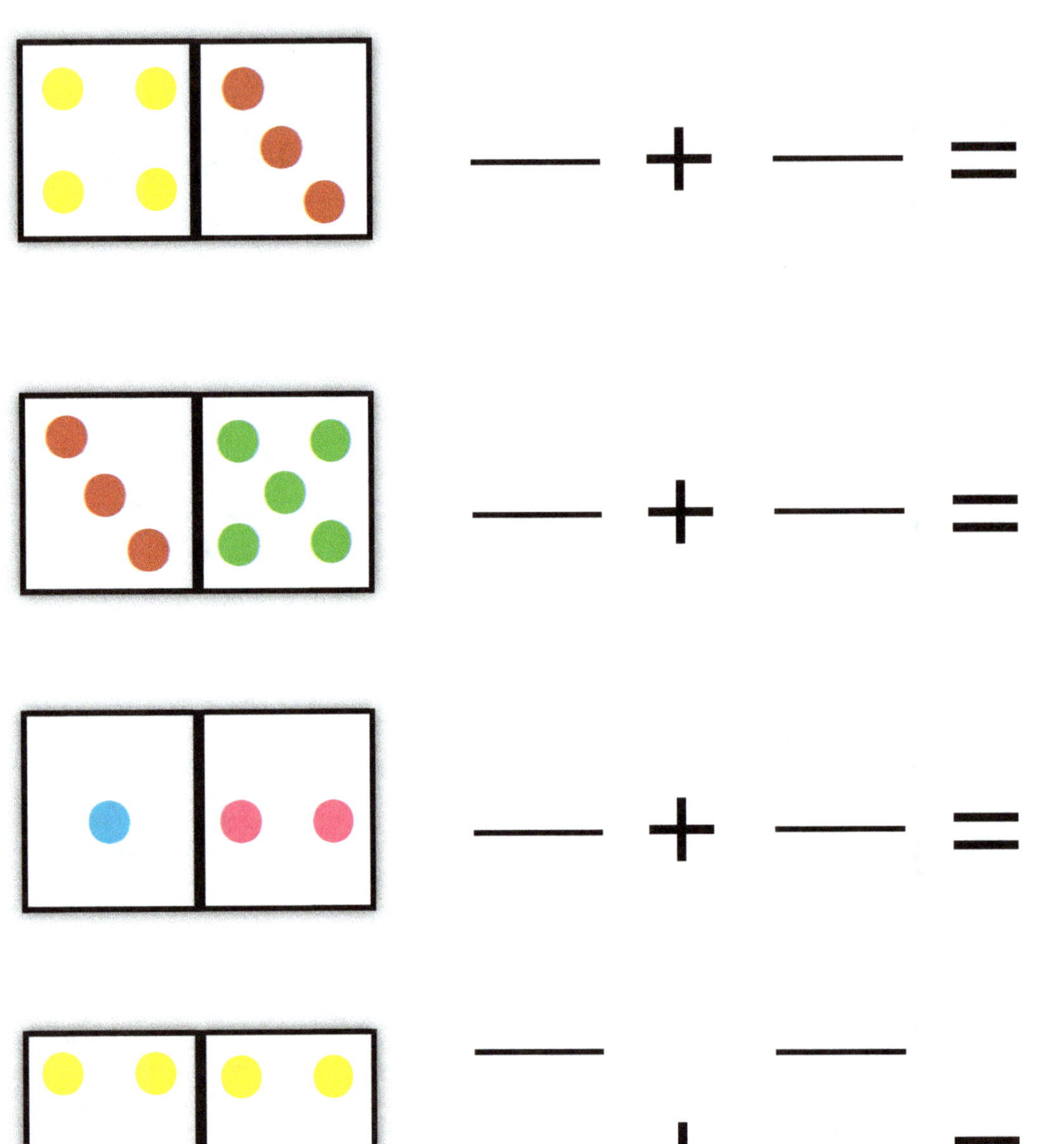

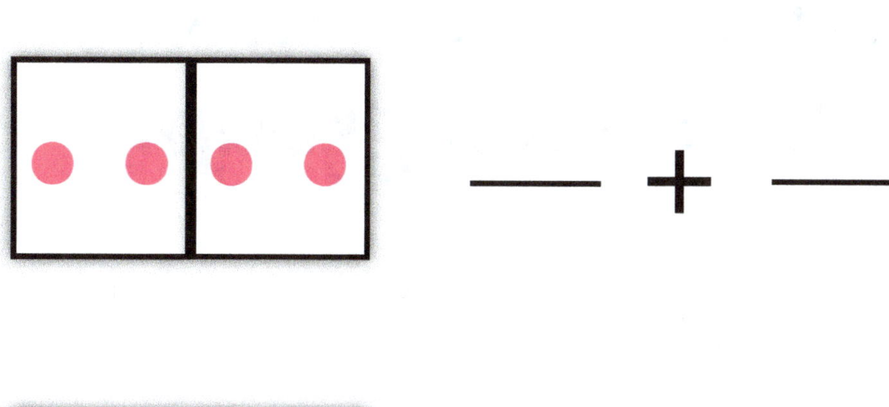

___ + ___ =

___ + ___ =

___ + ___ =

___ + ___ =

Draw more to make FIVE in each group.

5	
5	
5	

Draw more to make SIX in each group.

6	
6	
6	

Draw more to make SEVEN in each group.

7	
7	
7	

Draw more to make EIGHT in each group.

8	○○
8	□□□□□
8	▯▯▯

Draw more to make NINE in each group.

9	
9	
9	

What comes next?

1 2 ___

4 ___ 6

___ 8 9

What comes next?

2 ♡ 4 5 6

1 💬 3 4 5

6 ☐ 8 9 10

Connect each set with the number that goes with it

stop
hop

How many colors are there in the rainbow?

How many children are there in the picture?

How many corns do you see?

3
2
5
4
1

Circle the biggest.

Circle the smallest.

Simple Addition

+ =

+ =

+ =

$+ \quad =$

$+ \quad =$

+ =

Connect each set with the number that goes with it

• 7

• 4

• 8

• 4

• 5

• 8

• 6

• 7

• 2

Connect the dots by number order.

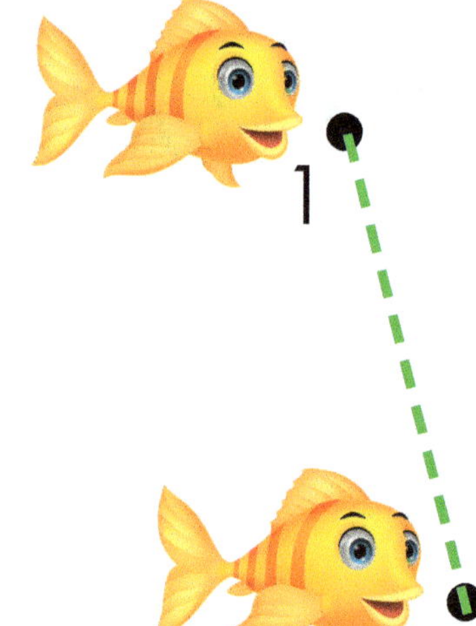

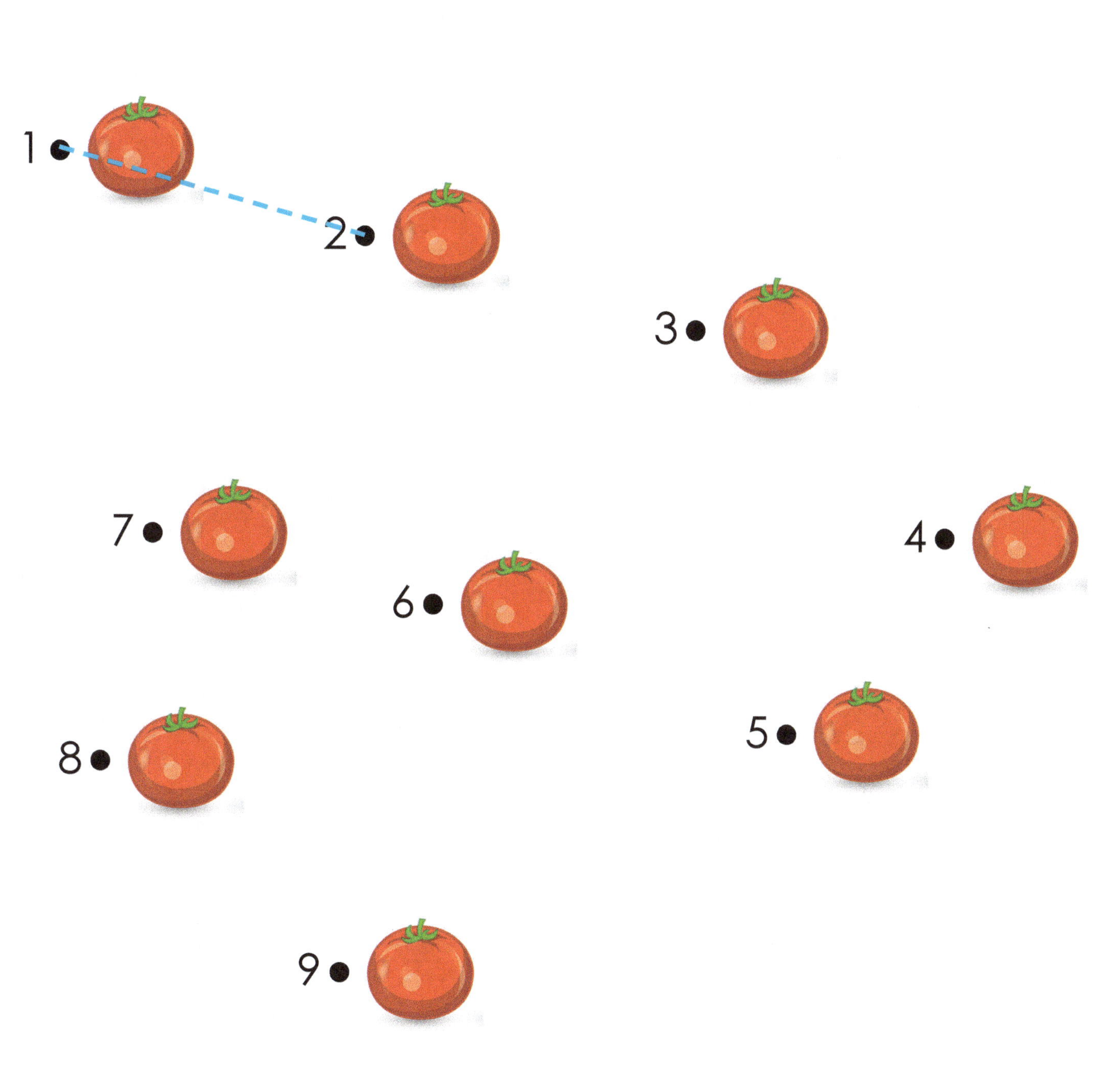
1
2
3
4
5
6
7
8
9